SWEETS &
CHOCOLATES

KÖNEMANN

Sweets & Chocolates

S weets and chocolates are possibly the
world's favourite foods and are almost as
much fun to make as they are to eat. In
this collection of recipes we show you how to
create some wonderful sweets and chocolates,
ranging from easy favourites for beginners to
more complicated delicacies for experienced
cooks. Before you start, read over these pages
to understand the how and why of making
your own sweets and chocolates.

*Place sugar thermometer
in the boiling sugar syrup
with the bulb submerged.*

sugar is very hot indeed
(see Note, next page).

Basics: Sweets

Making sweets is a
process that works
better if you obey the
rules. Follow the recipes
carefully and you'll find
they work beautifully.
Read through the recipe
before you begin and
assemble and prepare
the equipment and
ingredients. And, for
when you have finished,
storage details are given.

Working with syrups
cooking at high
temperatures means
that you must take
extra care. Stir hot
mixtures gently with a
wooden spoon and
avoid splashing.
Remove pans from heat
onto a wooden board
or a surface that won't
burn. Never touch the
pan or put your fingers
in the mixture, as hot

Equipment

Use a heavy-based pan
and the correct size as
stated in the recipe. A
sugar thermometer is an
invaluable tool because
it takes the guesswork
out of testing mixtures.
Choose one with large,
clear markings.

A wooden spoon
with a long handle will
not conduct heat, and is
still the best tool for

*Sugar syrup. Soft-ball stage: Sugar forms
soft ball that runs between your fingers .*

*Hard-ball stage: Sugar forms a firm ball
that will hold its shape.*

beating fudge. Other recipes may require an electric mixer.

A large marble slab is great for working with hot mixtures such as for making fondants or hard sweets, e.g. humbugs.

All the equipment we used in this book is readily available from cake-decorating stores, specialty kitchenware and department stores.

Making sugar syrup

Many sweets recipes begin with a boiled sugar syrup and it is important to follow the recipe. There are some simple rules for making successful sugar syrups:
◆ All sugar must be dissolved before the mixture boils.
◆ Keep the sides of the pan free from sugar crystals by brushing pan with a wet pastry brush. If crystals fall into the syrup it may crystallise.
◆ Do not stir the mixture after it boils unless specified in the recipe.
◆ Boil syrup to the correct temperature and remove the pan from the heat immediately.

Testing sugar syrup

There are two ways to test syrup temperature:
Using a sugar thermometer: Place the thermometer in the pan, with the bulb under the syrup's surface, after the sugar has come to the boil. Remove the pan from the heat as soon as the correct temperature has been reached.
Hand-testing: Dip a teaspoon (preferably with a long handle) into the boiling syrup to catch a small amount, and plunge it into a bowl or jug of ice-water. Knead the syrup in the water with your finger and thumb to form a ball.
◆ **Long-thread stage:** Temperature is 105°C. Forms a very soft thread between fingers.
◆ **Soft-ball stage:** Temperature is 115°C. Forms a soft ball that runs between your fingers.
◆ **Hard-ball stage:** Temperature is 122°C. Forms a firm ball that will hold its shape.
◆ **Small-crack stage:** Temperature is 138°C. Forms brittle yet sticky threads.
◆ **Hard-crack stage:** (Sometimes called crack stage) Temperature is

> **Note:** If you do get burnt, put the burn under cold water immediately and wash off the syrup. Keep burn immersed in cold water for 10 minutes.

Small-crack stage: The sugar forms a hard, yet sticky lump or threads.

Hard-crack stage: By this stage the sugar is very brittle and quite hard.

154°C. Forms very brittle, hard threads. After this stage, the mixture is too hot to test by hand.

Basics: Chocolates

Chocolate comes from the cocoa bean. To get from the tree to the candy bar is a long process. The beans are roasted and crushed, and the centre is ground to form a fatty liquid called chocolate liquor. This is rolled until it forms cocoa butter (which gives chocolate its yummy flavour and melting qualities) and cocoa cake, which becomes cocoa powder. The longer the chocolate is rolled the better and smoother the flavour.

As you read over our recipes, you'll notice that we specify the type of chocolate to use; not only white, dark or milk chocolate, but also compound or cooking or chocolate melts. That's because there are special types of chocolate that are each suited to particular tasks. Some are best for eating; some are formulated for cooking. Here we explain the types of chocolate we use in our recipes.

◆ **Compound chocolate:** This is the easiest chocolate to work with; it has other fats added to cocoa butter for that reason, and sets at room temperature. Excellent for dipping or coating. Choose a well-known brand for better flavour and quality. Chocolate melts are compound chocolate.

◆ **Cooking chocolate:** Excellent for cakes, sauces, icings, etc. Has a good rich flavour.

◆ **Dark chocolate:** Has a high cocoa-butter content and just enough sugar to be palatable.

◆ **Milk chocolate:** This is better for eating than cooking. It has a high sugar content, around 50 per cent, plus milk and chocolate liquor.

◆ **White chocolate:** The least stable type of chocolate to work with but good for giving a contrasting flavour and colour to other ingredients. It contains cocoa butter but no cocoa solids. It sets less firmly than other types.

Equipment

All the equipment used in these recipes is readily available from department, specialty kitchenware and cake-decorating stores.

◆ A piping bag is a tool that's often called for; here is a quick and easy way to make one:
Cut a 25 cm square of strong greaseproof paper and fold it in half to form a triangle.

For coating with chocolate: Use two forks, dip centres into melted chocolate.

After dipping, lift out and allow excess chocolate to drain.

For chocolate cups: Use a small brush to carefully paint the inside with chocolate.

To seal filled cups, pipe edge with chocolate; top with chocolate disc.

Working with the long side at the bottom, roll a corner to the centre and tape in place. Wrap the other corner around to the back and tape it in place. Fill with melted chocolate, fold the top, then roll down. Use scissors to snip off the tip of the bag to the size you need.

Working with chocolate

Before you begin melting chocolate, chop the block into smaller pieces. For chopping, use a large cooks' knife on a dry surface. If the weather is hot, refrigerate the chocolate briefly before chopping. The best results are achieved by working in a cool, dry room.

Chocolate should be melted gradually, otherwise it will burn – never melt it over direct heat. Instead, place the chocolate into a heatproof bowl and stand over a pan of gently simmering water, stirring until the chocolate is melted and is quite smooth. Or, you can use a double boiler. After it has melted, stir occasionally to stop the surface cooling.

If any water touches the chocolate while it is melting, it will "seize", becoming a hard, unworkable mass. If this happens, throw it away and start again.

The microwave can also be used to melt chocolate. Use short bursts of power to avoid "hot spots" which can burn the chocolate.

Melted chocolate can then be used in a variety of ways. You can dip nuts or other combined ingredients into it, to make an enormous variety of chocolate-coated goodies. Use two forks to dip each piece into the chocolate, lift up and let excess chocolate run back into the bowl, then place onto your prepared surface to dry.

To make dressy, elegant chocolates, line foil cases or other moulds by carefully painting them with a small brush dipped in melted chocolate. Turn upside down on a wire rack to set. When cool, they can be filled and the foil peeled off.

Storage
Uncooked chocolate should be stored at around 16°C in a dry place. If chocolate is kept at too warm a temperature it develops a white "bloom" of sugar on the surface. Wrap opened chocolate in foil or plastic wrap and store away from other foods.

5

Old-fashioned Favourites

Fudge, honeycomb, caramels and crunchy, nutty brittle have been lighting up the eyes of children (and adults) for many generations. Nowadays, refrigerators and food processors help us make these recipes easily and speedily, but it's still fun to wield a wooden spoon in the time-honoured tradition.

Tipsy Fudge

Preparation time:
  10 minutes
Cooking time:
  25 minutes
Makes 36 pieces

3/4 cup sultanas
2 tablespoons rum
3 cups sugar
2 tablespoons glucose
  syrup
1 cup milk
90 g unsalted butter

1 Brush a 20 cm square cake tin with melted butter or oil. Line the base and sides with foil; grease foil.
2 Combine the sultanas and rum, set aside.
3 Combine the sugar, glucose syrup and milk in a large, heavy-based pan. Stir over medium heat without boiling until the sugar has completely dissolved. Brush the sugar crystals from sides of pan with a wet pastry brush. Bring to the boil, reduce heat slightly, boil without stirring for about 20 minutes; OR boil until a teaspoon of mixture dropped into cold water reaches soft-ball stage (see page 3); OR if using a sugar thermometer it must reach 115°C (see page 3). Remove from heat immediately.
4 Add butter to pan, without stirring. Stand 5 minutes, then add the sultanas and beat until thick and creamy. Pour into prepared tin and leave to cool. Cut into squares when cold. Store in an airtight container in a cool dark place for up to 1 week.

Clockwise from top left: Turkish Delight (p. 8), Tipsy Fudge and Honeycomb (p. 9).

1. For Turkish Delight: Combine rinds, juices, sugar and water in pan.

2. Brush sugar crystals from the side of the pan with a wet pastry brush.

Turkish Delight

Preparation time:
  30 minutes +
  overnight setting
Cooking time:
  20 minutes
Makes 50

rind of 1 medium lemon
rind of 1 medium
  orange
1/4 cup orange juice
2 tablespoons lemon
  juice
3 cups caster sugar
1/2 cup water
2 tablespoons gelatine
1 cup water, extra
2/3 cup cornflour
3-4 drops orange or
  rose flower water
red food colouring
1/2 cup icing sugar

1 Line the base and sides of a deep 17 cm square cake tin with aluminium foil, leaving the edges overhanging. Brush the foil with melted butter or oil.

2 Remove any white pith from the lemon and orange rinds. Combine rinds, juices, sugar and water in large heavy-based pan. Stir over medium heat without boiling until sugar has completely dissolved. Brush sugar crystals from the side of pan with a wet pastry brush. Bring to boil, reduce heat slightly and boil without stirring for about 5 minutes; OR boil until a teaspoon of mixture dropped into cold water forms long threads (see page 3); OR if using a sugar thermometer it must reach 105°C (see page 3). Remove from heat immediately.

3 Combine the gelatine with 1/2 cup of extra water in a small glass bowl. Stir over hot water until dissolved. In a separate small bowl combine cornflour with the remaining water and mix until smooth.

4 Add the gelatine and cornflour mixtures to the sugar syrup. Stir over medium heat until mixture boils and clears. Stir in the flower water and a few drops of red food colouring.

5 Strain mixture into prepared tin; smooth surface. Refrigerate overnight. When set, lift from tin using foil. Carefully peel off foil. Cut into squares with a sharp knife. Roll squares in icing sugar. Store Turkish Delight between layers of greaseproof paper in an airtight container.

HINT
Caster sugar is a superfine cane sugar that dissolves quickly in mixing and baking. Caster sugar is also perfect for meringues, although soft brown sugar can be used to give a chewy texture.

3. Add the gelatine and cornflour mixture to the sugar syrup.

4. Strain mixture into prepared tin. When set cut into squares.

Honeycomb

Preparation time:
  10 minutes +
  1½ hours setting
Cooking time:
  23 minutes
Makes about 28 pieces

1¾ cups sugar
¼ cup glucose liquid
½ cup water
2 teaspoons bicarbonate
  of soda

1 Line base and sides of a 27 x 18 cm oblong tin with aluminium foil; brush the foil with melted butter or oil.
2 Combine the sugar, glucose and water in a large, heavy-based pan. Stir over medium heat without boiling until sugar has completely dissolved. Brush sugar crystals from sides of pan with a wet pastry brush. Bring to the boil, reduce heat slightly, boil without stirring for about 8 minutes or until the mixture just begins to turn golden. Remove from heat immediately.
3 Add the sifted soda to the sugar mixture. Using a wooden spoon, stir until bubbles begin to subside and there is no soda visible on the surface of the mixture.
4 Pour carefully into prepared tin and leave to set, about 1½ hours. Remove from tin, peel away foil and cut into pieces. Store in an airtight container in a cool dark place, for up to 7 days.

> ### HINT
> When sweet-making, place the prepared tin in the position you intend to leave it to set before pouring in the hot mixture. Do not touch tin for at least 30 minutes, as it will be extremely hot.

Buttered Brazil Nuts

Preparation time:
  10 minutes
Cooking time:
  30 minutes
Makes about 24

2 cups sugar
½ cup water
2 tablespoons liquid
  glucose
125g unsalted butter
1 tablespoon white
  vinegar
2 cups (250g) whole
  Brazil nuts

1 Line two 32 x 28 cm oven trays with foil, brush foil with melted butter or oil.
2 Combine the sugar, water, liquid glucose, butter and vinegar in a medium, heavy-based pan. Stir over medium heat without boiling until butter has melted and sugar has completely

dissolved. Brush sugar crystals from sides of pan with a wet pastry brush. Bring to the boil, reduce heat slightly, boil without stirring for about 25 minutes; OR boil until a teaspoon of the mixture dropped into cold water reaches soft-crack stage (see page 3); OR if using a sugar thermometer it must reach 138°C (see page 3). Remove from heat immediately.

3 Using a wooden spoon, dip whole nuts into the butterscotch mixture. Place onto prepared trays to set. Store between sheets of waxed paper in an airtight container at room temperature for up to 7 days.

Note: While Brazil nuts are traditionally used in this recipe, different types of nuts or a combination may be used. Use the quantity given (by weight); if using smaller nuts dip a few at a time to form clusters.

Fruit Jellies
Preparation time:
  10 minutes
Cooking time:
  5 minutes +
  2 hours setting
Makes 40

200 mL lemon or
  orange juice, strained
2 tablespoons sugar
¼ cup glucose syrup
40 g gelatine
100 mL water

1 Line base and sides of a 20 cm square cake tin with aluminium foil.
2 Combine juice, sugar and glucose syrup in a medium pan. Stir over medium heat until the sugar and glucose have dissolved. Remove from heat; leave to cool until just warm.
3 Combine the gelatine with water in a small bowl. Stand bowl in hot water; stir until gelatine dissolves. Pour slowly into the juice mixture, stirring constantly (see Note). Pour mixture into prepared tin and leave to set at room temperature. (In hot weather you may have to refrigerate the mixture to set it.)
5 When set, remove from the tin. Using a long sharp knife cut the sides neatly away from the foil. Turn onto a board, carefully peel off

the foil and cut jelly into diamond shapes. Store Fruit Jellies in an airtight container in a cool, dark place, or in the refrigerator in hot weather, for up to 4 days.

Note: To avoid lumps forming, it is important that the gelatine solution and the juice mixture are the same temperature when they are mixed together.

Cobbers
Preparation time:
  20 minutes +
  2 hours setting
Cooking time:
  30 minutes
Makes about 40

1¼ cups sugar
1¼ cup cream
2 tablespoons light corn
  syrup
60 g unsalted butter
180 g dark compound
  chocolate, chopped

1 Line base and sides of a 21 x 14 cm loaf tin with aluminium foil; brush foil with melted butter or oil.
2 Combine the sugar, cream, corn syrup and butter in a medium, heavy-based pan. Stir over medium heat without boiling until the butter has melted and the sugar has completely dissolved. Brush sugar

Clockwise from top: Buttered Brazil Nuts (p. 9), Fruit Jellies and Cobbers.

crystals from sides of pan with a wet pastry brush. Bring to the boil, reduce heat slightly and boil without stirring for about 20 minutes; OR boil until a teaspoon of the mixture dropped into cold water reaches hard-ball stage (see page 3); OR if using a sugar thermometer it must reach 122°C (see page 3). Remove from heat immediately.

3 Pour into prepared tin and leave to cool. While the caramel is still warm mark squares about 1 cm; when cold, cut into cubes.

4 Line a 32 x 28 cm oven tray with aluminium foil. Place the chocolate in a small heatproof bowl. Stand over pan of simmering water, stir until the chocolate has melted and is smooth. Remove

from heat. Cool slightly. Using two forks, dip caramels one at a time in chocolate to coat. Lift out, drain excess chocolate, then place onto the prepared tray. Leave to set. Store Cobbers in an airtight container in a cool dark place for up to 4 weeks.

Note: Pipe stripes of melted dark chocolate onto the tops, if liked.

11

Caramels

Preparation time:
  10 minutes + 30
  minutes refrigeration
Cooking time:
  20 minutes
Makes 36

125 g butter
400 g can condensed
  milk
1 cup caster sugar
1/2 cup golden syrup

1 Line base and sides
of a shallow 17 cm
square cake tin with
foil, leaving edges
overhanging. Brush foil
with melted butter or oil.
2 Combine the butter,
condensed milk, caster
sugar and golden syrup
in a medium, heavy-
based pan. Stir over low
heat without boiling
until the sugar has
completely dissolved.
Bring to the boil and
reduce heat slightly. Stir
constantly for about
15-20 minutes, until
mixture turns a dark
golden caramel colour
(see Note).
3 Pour the mixture into
the prepared tin; smooth
surface. Using a sharp
knife, mark caramel
into squares. Refrigerate
30 minutes or until firm.
Remove from tin; cut
through. Store Caramels
in an airtight container
in the refrigerator up to
3 weeks.

Note: Constant stirring
while the caramel is
cooking will prevent the
bottom burning. If heat
is too high the mixture
will burn quickly. If the
caramel is not cooked
long enough it will not
set properly and will be
very soft and sticky.

Peanut Brittle

Preparation time:
  20 minutes
Cooking time:
  15 minutes
Makes about 500 g

2 cups sugar
1 cup brown sugar,
  lightly packed
1/2 cup golden syrup
1/2 cup water
60 g butter
2 1/2 cups roasted,
  unsalted peanuts

1 Line base and sides
of a shallow 30 x 25 x
2 cm Swiss roll tin with
foil or greaseproof
paper. Brush foil with
melted butter or oil.
2 Combine sugars,
syrup and water in a
large heavy-based pan.
Stir over medium heat
without boiling until
sugar has completely
dissolved. Brush sugar
crystals from the side of
pan with a wet pastry
brush. Add butter, stir
until melted. Bring to
the boil, reduce heat
slightly and boil

without stirring for
about 15-20 minutes;
OR boil until a teaspoon
of mixture dropped into
cold water reaches soft-
crack stage (see page 3);
OR if using a sugar
thermometer it must
reach 138°C (see page 3).
Remove pan from heat
immediately.
3 Add peanuts. Using a
wooden spooon fold in
lightly, tilting pan from
side to side to help mix.
Pour mixture into the
prepared tin; smooth
surface using a buttered
metal spatula.
4 Stand on wire rack to
cool; break into pieces
when almost set. Store
Brittle in an airtight
container in a cool, dry
place for up to 3 weeks.

Note: Substitute any
roasted, unsalted nuts for
peanuts in this recipe.

Cherry Nougat Bites

Preparation time:
  30 minutes
Cooking time: Nil
Makes 26

1/4 cup condensed milk
1 teaspoon imitation
  vanilla essence
1 tablespoon brown
  sugar
3/4 cup powdered milk
2/3 cup glacé cherries,
  chopped

From left: Cherry Nougat Bites, Peanut Brittle and Caramels.

1 Combine condensed milk, vanilla and sugar in a medium mixing bowl. Stir in powdered milk and cherries. Using a wooden spoon stir until combined.
2 Turn mixture onto surface lightly dusted with icing sugar. Knead until smooth. Divide the mixture in half. Roll each half between the palms of hands into a rope 2.5 cm thick. Dust with extra icing sugar. Refrigerate until firm. When firm cut into 2.5 cm pieces. Store in an airtight container in the refrigerator for up to 2 weeks.

Note. Try using a combination of glacé cherries and chopped nuts in this recipe.

13

Chocolate Florentines

Preparation time:
 40 minutes
Cooking time:
 10 minutes
Makes 34

50 g butter
2 tablespoons dark
 brown sugar
1 tablespoon plain flour
1 cup cornflakes
2 tablespoons chopped
 glacé cherries
2 tablespoons mixed
 peel
100 g dark cooking
 chocolate, chopped

1 Preheat oven to moderate 180°C. Brush a 32 x 38 cm oven tray with melted butter or oil, line base with paper; grease paper.
2 Combine butter and sugar in medium heavy-based pan. Stir over low heat until butter has melted and the sugar is completely dissolved. Remove from heat.
3 Add the plain flour, cornflakes, cherries and the mixed peel to pan. Using a wooden spoon, stir until the mixture is just combined.

Clockwise from left: Chocolate Florentines, Marzipan Fruits, Rum Balls and Peppermint Humbugs (pps. 16, 17).

15

Drop teaspoons of the mixture onto prepared trays, allowing room for spreading. Bake for 10 minutes or until crisp and lightly browned. Cool on trays.

4 Place chocolate in a small heatproof bowl. Stand over pan of simmering water, stir until melted and smooth; remove from heat. Cool slightly. Spread chocolate over base of florentines with a flat-bladed knife. Place upside down on a wire rack until set. Store in an airtight container in a cool, dry place for up to 2 weeks.

Note: Substitute a mixture of chopped glacé fruits for cherries in this recipe, if desired.

Peppermint Humbugs

Preparation time:
 1 hour
Cooking time:
 15 minutes
Makes about 30

2 cups sugar
1/4 cup water
50 g butter
1 tablespoon liquid
 glucose
peppermint essence
 or oil
green food colouring

1 Brush a large marble slab or board with oil.
2 Combine the sugar, water, butter and glucose in large heavy-based pan. Stir over medium heat without boiling until sugar has completely dissolved. Brush sugar crystals from the side of pan with a wet pastry brush. Bring to boil,

reduce heat slightly, boil without stirring for about 15 minutes; OR boil until a teaspoon of mixture dropped into cold water reaches small-crack stage (see page 3); OR if using a sugar thermometer it must reach 138°C (see page 3). Remove from heat immediately. Leave to cool slightly.

3 Pour mixture onto marble slab; add a few drops of essence and colour. When mixture begins to cool, using a spatula, turn the edges towards the centre. Repeat until mixture is cool enough to handle.

3 Pull toffee into long strips, twist together and pull out again. Repeat until toffee begins to harden and whiten. Using scissors, cut into 2 cm pieces. Leave on slab to harden. Store in an airtight containter in a cool dry place for up to 2 weeks.

1. *For Peppermint Humbugs: Combine sugar, water, butter and glucose.*

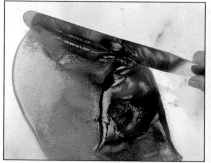

2. *When mixture begins to cool, turn the edges towards the centre.*

Marzipan Fruits

Preparation time:
 1 hour
Cooking time:
 Nil
Makes about 10-12

200 g ground almonds
1 cup icing sugar, sifted
1 egg white, lightly
 beaten
1/2 teaspoon liquid
 glucose
flavoured essence,
 optional
food colourings

1 Combine almonds and sugar in a medium mixing bowl. Make a well in the centre. Add combined egg white and glucose. Using a wooden spoon, stir until well combined. Add flavour if desired. Turn onto work surface lightly sprinkled with icing sugar, knead for 5 minutes or until fairly dry and smooth. Cover with plastic wrap; refrigerate 15 minutes.
2 Break off 10-12 pieces of marzipan. Mould into fruit shapes: bananas, oranges, apples, grapes and pears. Place on a tray. Leave to dry. Paint fruits with appropriate food colouring to finish. Leave to dry. Store, covered, in refrigerator for up to 4 weeks.

Rum Balls

Preparation time:
 40 minutes
Cooking time:
 3 minutes
Makes 30

250 g chocolate cake,
 crumbled
1/4 cup ground walnuts
1 tablespoon golden
 syrup
1 tablespoon overproof
 rum
80 g butter
1 tablespoon blackberry
 jam
50 g dark chocolate,
 grated
1/2 cup chocolate
 sprinkles

1 Line a 32 x 28 cm oven tray with foil.
2 Combine the cake crumbs, walnuts, syrup and rum in medium mixing bowl. Make a well in the centre.
3 Combine the butter and jam in a small pan. Stir over low heat until melted; remove from heat.
4 Add butter mixture to cake crumbs. Using a wooden spoon, stir until the mixture is just combined. Add grated chocolate; mix well.
5 Using hands, roll two teaspoons of mixture into a ball. Roll in sprinkles; place onto prepared tray and refrigerate until firm. Repeat with remaining mixture. Store Rum Balls in an airtight container in refrigerator for up to 3 weeks.

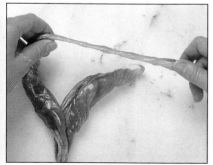

3. Pull and twist toffee until it begins to harden and whiten.

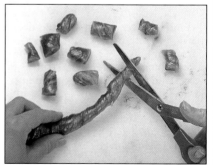

4. Cut toffee into 2 cm pieces. Leave on marble slab to harden.

Fête Fare

There's always a rush to the home-made sweet stall at fêtes and these recipes will be sure to entice crowds to your worthy cause. Package your goodies in see-through paper and ribbon; marshmallows and other soft sweets may need a firmer base such as a doily-covered paper plate. Save a few to display in baskets or trays for individual sale. Most of these recipes can be made up to two weeks ahead.

Small Toffees

Preparation time:
  10 minutes
Cooking time:
  25 minutes
Makes about 24

4 *cups sugar*
1 *cup water*
1 *tablespoon vinegar*
hundreds and
  thousands or
  desiccated coconut for
  decoration

1 Line two deep 12-cup patty tins with paper patty cases.
2 Combine the sugar, water and vinegar in a large, heavy-based pan (see Note). Stir over medium heat without boiling until sugar has completely dissolved. Brush sugar crystals from sides of pan with a wet pastry brush. Bring to the boil, reduce heat slightly, boil without stirring for about 20 minutes; OR boil until a teaspoon of mixture dropped into cold water reaches small-crack stage (see page 3); OR if using a sugar thermometer it must reach 138°C (see page 3). Remove from heat immediately.
3 Pour into patty cases and decorate as desired. Leave to set at room temperature. Store Toffees in an airtight container in a cool dry place for up to 7 days.

Note: Using a heavy-based pan ensures that the toffee will not burn.

Clockwise from top: Toffee Apples, Toasted Marshmallows (p. 20) and Small Toffees.

1. *For Toffee Apples: Push a wooden icy-pole stick into apple stem.*

2. *Add cream of tartar and red food colouring to the sugar mixture.*

Toffee Apples

Preparation time:
  15 minutes
Cooking time:
  20 minutes
Makes 15

15 small red apples,
  very crisp
4 cups sugar
1 cup water
1/2 teaspoon cream of
  tartar
3 teaspoons red food
  colouring

1 Line a 32 x 28 cm oven tray with foil. Brush the foil with melted butter or oil.
2 Wipe the apples thoroughly with a clean, dry towel. Push a wooden icy-pole stick or thick skewer into the stem of each apple.
3 Combine sugar and water in a large, heavy-based pan. Stir over medium heat without boiling until sugar has completely dissolved. Brush crystals from side of pan with a wet pastry brush. Add the cream of tartar and food colouring. Bring to the boil, reduce heat slightly, boil without stirring for about 15 minutes; OR boil until a teaspoon of mixture dropped into cold water reaches small-crack stage (see page 3); OR if using a sugar thermometer it must reach 138°C (see page 3). Remove from heat immediately.
4 Twist apples, one at a time, into syrup to coat. Drain and place onto the prepared baking tray. Leave to set at room temperature. Wrap in cellophane and tie with a ribbon. Toffee apples will keep up to 2 days.

Note: Wooden icy-pole sticks are available from some newsagents or stationery stockists.

Toasted Marshmallows

Preparation time:
  25 minutes
Cooking time:
  3 minutes
Makes 36

1 1/2 cups caster sugar
1/2 cup water
5 teaspoons gelatine
1/2 cup water, extra
1 teaspoon imitation
  vanilla essence
3/4 cup desiccated
  coconut

1 Line a shallow 30 x 20 cm oblong cake tin with aluminium foil; brush foil with melted butter or oil.
2 Using electric beaters, beat sugar and water in a large mixing bowl for 3 minutes.
3 Combine the gelatine with water in a small bowl. Stand bowl in hot water; stir until dissolved.

3. If using a sugar thermometer, it must reach 138°C.

4. Twist apples, one at a time, into sugar syrup to coat.

Add to sugar mixture. Using electric beaters, beat for 10 minutes, until the mixture is thick and white. Add essence. Pour into prepared tin and spread out evenly. Leave overnight to set at room temperature.
4 Preheat oven to moderate 180°C. Spread the coconut evenly on a flat baking tray. Bake for about 3 minutes, or until golden (see Note). Pour onto a plate to cool.
5 Turn marshmallow out of tin and cut into cubes. Place the toasted coconut in a plastic bag and add a few cubes of marshmallow at a time. Shake to coat. Repeat with remaining cubes. Store in a single layer in an airtight container in a cool dark place for up to 7 days. Keep flat.

Note: Watch coconut carefully when toasting as it will brown quickly once it begins to colour.

Rocky Road

Preparation time:
  10 minutes
Cooking time:
  5 minutes
Makes about 36 pieces

1/4 cup desiccated
  coconut
100 g packet white
  marshmallows
100 g packet pink
  marshmallows
1/2 cup mixed, unsalted
  nuts
375 g milk chocolate
  melts

1 Line base and sides of a shallow 27 x 18 cm cake tin with foil.
2 Sprinkle half the coconut over the base of the prepared tin.
3 Cut marshmallows in half and arrange in tin in alternating colours, leaving space between the pieces. Sprinkle the remaining coconut and nuts between the marshmallows and around edge of tin.
4 Place the chocolate in a medium heatproof bowl. Stand over a pan of simmering water, stir until the chocolate has melted and is smooth. Cool slightly.
5 Pour chocolate into gaps and around edges of marshmallows. Leave to set. Using a sharp knife, cut into pieces. Store in an airtight container in a cool dark place for up to 2 weeks.

HINT
Amaranth powder is a red colouring once used by pharmacists in the preparation of medications. Use a little to colour toffee apples for a really professional look. Your local chemist may stock it. Or try using the red food colouring powder from Asian stores.

21

Pecan Buttermilk Drops

Preparation time:
  10 minutes +
  2 hours setting
Cooking time:
  25 minutes
Makes about 24

2 cups brown sugar
1½ cups buttermilk
90 g unsalted butter,
  cubed
250 g pecans, roughly
  chopped
1 teaspoon vanilla
  essence

1 Line a 32 x 28 cm oven tray with foil.
2 Combine the brown sugar and buttermilk in a large heavy-based pan. Stir over medium heat without boiling until the sugar has completely dissolved. Brush sugar crystals from sides of pan with a wet pastry brush. Bring to the boil, reduce heat slightly and boil without stirring for 20 minutes; OR boil until a teaspoon of the mixture dropped into cold water reaches soft-ball stage (see page 3); OR if using a sugar thermometer it must reach 115°C. (see page 3). Remove from heat immediately. Add butter and set aside to cool without stirring for 15 minutes.
3 Add chopped pecans and vanilla to the cooled mixture. Using a wooden spoon, beat briskly 3 minutes. Drop heaped teaspoons of the mixture onto the prepared tray. Leave to set at room temperature. (This is a soft candy and will not set hard.) Store in an airtight container in a cool dry place for up to 7 days.

Penuche

Preparation time:
  15 minutes +
  2½ hours setting
Cooking time:
  30 minutes
Makes 36 squares

400 g brown sugar
1¼ cups cream
1 teaspoon vanilla
  essence

1 Line base and sides of a 20 cm square cake tin with aluminium foil extending over two sides. Brush foil with melted butter or oil.
2 Combine sugar and cream in a medium, heavy-based pan. Stir over medium heat without boiling until sugar has completely dissolved. Brush sugar crystals from sides of pan with a wet pastry brush. Bring to the boil, reduce heat slightly, boil without stirring for 25 minutes; OR boil until a teaspoon of the mixture dropped into cold water reaches soft-ball stage (see page 3); OR if using a sugar thermometer it must reach 115°C (see page 3). Remove from heat immediately.
3 Set aside to cool in pan for 30 minutes. Add vanilla essence. Using a wooden spoon, beat for 5 minutes.
4 Press into prepared tin; smooth surface and score into 2 cm squares. Leave to set at room temperature, about 2 hours. Using foil, lift out of tin and cut into squares. Store Penuche in an airtight container in a cool dark place for up to 2 weeks.

Note: Penuche is based on a traditional sweet from Mexico. It is pronounced *pen-oo-shee*.

> **HINT**
> A long-handled wooden spoon is ideal for stirring hot sugar mixtures. Never use electric beaters to mix fudge or penuche because the thick mixture will overtax the motor.

Clockwise from left: Penuche, Rocky Road (p. 21), and Pecan Buttermilk Drops.

Crunchy Peanut Squares

Preparation time:
  15 minutes +
  2 hours refrigeration
Cooking time:
  5 minutes
Makes about 40

250 g packet chocolate
  cream biscuits
65 g unsalted peanuts
  (optional)
150 g dark compound
  chocolate
60 g unsalted butter
½ cup smooth peanut
  butter

1 Line base and sides
of a shallow 27 x 18 cm
oblong cake tin with
foil; brush foil with
melted butter or oil.
2 Place the biscuits in a
strong plastic bag and
break up with a rolling
pin. Do not crush too
finely. Place crumbs in a
large mixing bowl with
the peanuts, if using.
3 Combine chocolate,
butter and peanut butter
in a medium pan and
stir over low heat until
butter is melted and the
mixture is smooth and
well combined. Pour
onto the crumb mixture;
stir until well combined.
Press into the prepared
tin, using the back of a
metal spoon to smooth
the surface. Refrigerate
for 2 hours or until firm.

4 Remove slice from
tin. Peel off foil. Using a
sharp knife, cut into
squares. Store in an
airtight container in a
cool dark place, or in
the refrigerator in hot
weather, up to 7 days.

Toffee Muesli Bars

Preparation time:
  10 minutes
Cooking time:
  25 minutes
Makes 24

1 cup sugar
2 tablespoons honey
2 tablespoons glucose
  syrup
50 g unsalted butter
⅓ cup water
400 g untoasted muesli

1 Line base and sides
of a shallow 27 x 18 cm
oblong cake tin with
foil. Brush foil with
melted butter or oil.
2 Combine the sugar,
honey, glucose, butter
and water in a medium
heavy-based pan. Stir
over medium heat
without boiling until
sugar has completely
dissolved. Brush sugar
crystals from sides of
pan with a wet pastry
brush. Bring to the boil,
reduce heat slightly, boil
without stirring for
20 minutes; OR boil
until a teaspoon of
mixture dropped into
cold water reaches hard-

ball stage (see page 3);
OR if using a sugar
thermometer it must
reach 122°C (see page
3). Remove pan from
heat immediately.
3 Place the muesli in a
large warmed mixing
bowl (not plastic). Pour
in toffee mixture and
quickly stir to combine.
Pour into the prepared
tin and smooth surface
with the back of a
metal spoon. Score into
24 bars while warm;
cut through when cold.
Store in an airtight
container in a cool,
dark place up to 7 days.

Coconut Ice

Preparation time:
  30 minutes
Cooking time:
  Nil
Makes 30 pieces

2½ cups icing sugar
¼ teaspoon cream of
  tartar
1 egg white, lightly
  beaten
¼ cup condensed milk
1¾ cups desiccated
  coconut
pink food colouring

1 Brush a 26 x 8 x
4.5 cm bar tin with
melted butter or oil.
Line the base with
paper; grease paper.
2 Sift the icing sugar
and cream of tartar into
a medium mixing bowl;

Clockwise from left: Toffee Muesli Bars, Crunchy Peanut Squares and Coconut Ice.

make a well in the centre. Add the combined egg white and condensed milk. Using a wooden spoon, stir in half the coconut. Add the remaining coconut. Using your hand, mix until well combined. Divide the mixture into two bowls. Tint one half of mixture with pink colouring. Using your hand, knead colour evenly through.

3 Press pink mixture over base of prepared tin; cover with the white mixture and press down evenly. Refrigerate 1 hour or until set. When firm, remove from tin and cut into squares. Store in an airtight container in a cool dark place for up to 2 weeks.

Note: For extra flavour, add strawberry essence or oil to the pink mixture.

25

Easy Chocolate Fudge

Preparation time:
  10 minutes
Cooking time:
  5 minutes
Makes 64

125 g dark cooking
  chocolate, chopped
125 g unsalted butter
1½ cups icing sugar,
  sifted
2 tablespoons milk
½ cup coarsely
  chopped pecans,
  almonds, walnuts or
  hazelnuts

1 Line base and sides of a shallow 17 cm square cake tin with aluminium foil. Brush the foil with melted butter or oil.
2 Combine chocolate, butter, sugar and milk in a medium heavy-based pan. Stir over low heat until chocolate and butter have melted and the mixture is smooth. Bring to boil; boil for 1 minute only. Remove from heat; beat with a wooden spoon until mixture is smooth. Fold in the chopped nuts.
3 Pour the mixture into prepared tin; smooth surface with the back of a metal spoon. Stand

tin on wire rack to cool. When firm, remove from tin. Carefully peel off foil and cut into squares. Store Easy Chocolate Fudge in an airtight container in a cool, dark place for up to 7 days.

Choc-Top Caramel Fudge

Preparation time:
  20 minutes
Cooking time:
  20 minutes
Makes 36

2 cups sugar
1 cup milk
⅔ cup cream
¼ cup light corn syrup
1 teaspoon vanilla
  essence
80 g dark cooking
  chocolate, chopped

1 Line base and sides of a deep 20 cm square cake tin with aluminium foil. Brush foil with butter or oil.
2 Combine sugar, milk, cream and corn syrup in a large heavy-based

pan. Stir over medium heat without boiling until sugar has completely dissolved. Brush sugar crystals from the side of pan with a wet pastry brush. Bring to boil, reduce heat slightly and boil without stirrring for 15 minutes; OR boil until a teaspoon of mixture dropped into cold water reaches soft-ball stage (see page 3); OR if using a sugar thermometer it must reach 115°C (see page 3). Remove from heat immediately.
3 Cool for 5 minutes. Add vanilla essence; beat vigorously with a wooden spoon for 5 minutes or until the mixture begins to thicken and lose its gloss. Pour mixture into prepared tin; smooth surface. Stand on wire rack to cool.
4 Place chocolate in a small heatproof bowl. Stand over pan of simmering water, stir until chocolate has melted and is smooth. Cool slightly. Spread chocolate evenly over the fudge using a flat-bladed knife. Leave to set. When firm, remove from tin. Carefully peel off foil and cut into squares. Store in an airtight container in a cool, dark place for up to 2 weeks.

Easy Chocolate Fudge (top), Choc-Top Caramel Fudge (bottom).

Caramel Popcorn Balls

Preparation time:
  20 minutes
Cooking time:
  10 minutes
Makes 50 balls

2 tablespoons oil
1/2 cup popping corn
3/4 cup sugar
80 g unsalted butter
2 tablespoons honey
2 tablespoons cream

1 Heat oil in a large pan over medium heat. Add popping corn and cover tightly. Hold the lid of the pan on tightly and shake occasionally. Cook until the popping sounds stop. Put the popcorn into a large bowl; set aside.

2 Combine the sugar, butter, honey and cream in a small heavy-based pan. Stir over medium heat without boiling until the sugar has completely dissolved. Brush sugar crystals from sides of pan with a wet pastry brush. Bring to the boil and boil without stirring for 5 minutes.

3 Pour the syrup over the popcorn. Using 2 metal spoons combine thoroughly with the popcorn. When mixture has cooled enough to handle but not set, form popcorn into balls about the size of a golf ball with oiled hands. Place on wire rack to set. Store in an airtight container in a cool dark place for up to 1 week.

Note. Take care when handling the hot caramel mixture. It must be warm enough to be pliable, but not too hot to burn hands.

Caramel Popcorn Balls.

1. For Caramel Popcorn Balls: Add corn to pan and cover. Shake occasionally.

2. Combine sugar, butter, honey and cream in a small heavy-based pan.

3. *Pour syrup over popcorn. Combine thoroughly using two metal spoons.*

4. *With oiled hands, form popcorn into balls about the size of a golf ball.*

Apricot and Gingernut Logs

Preparation time:
40 minutes
Cooking time:
Nil
Makes 24

1/2 *cup roasted unsalted peanuts*
1/2 *cup crunchy peanut butter*
85 g dried apricots
50 g glacé ginger
2 tablespoons icing sugar
2 tablespoons flaked almonds
50 g dark compound chocolate, chopped

1 Place peanuts, peanut butter, apricots, ginger and icing sugar in food processor bowl. Using the pulse action, press button 15-20 seconds or until the mixture is smooth and lump-free.
2 Using hands, roll 2 teaspoons of mixture into small log shapes; place on a tray. Arrange almonds to overlap on the top of each log.
3 Place chocolate in a small heatproof bowl. Stand over a pan of simmering water, stir until the chocolate has melted and mixture is smooth. Cool slightly. Drizzle chocolate over logs in a zig-zag pattern. Refrigerate until firm.

Store the Apricot and Gingernut Logs in an airtight container for up to 2 weeks.

Note. Try rolling logs in crushed nuts before drizzling with chocolate.

Coconut Peach Bars

Preparation time:
40 minutes + 2 hours refrigeration
Cooking time:
15 minutes
Makes 40

250 g dried peaches
1 teaspoon grated orange rind
1/2 *cup orange juice*
2 tablespoons brown sugar
50 g unsalted butter
100 g packet white marshmallows
1/3 *cup desiccated coconut*
2 tablespoons oatmeal
1/4 *cup malted milk powder*
1/2 *cup powdered milk*
2/3 *cup desiccated coconut, extra*

1 Line the base and sides of a shallow 18 x 27 cm oblong cake tin with aluminium foil. Brush the foil with melted butter or oil.

2 Combine the peaches, rind, juice and sugar in a medium heavy-based pan. Stir over low heat until the sugar has completely dissolved. Bring to boil, reduce heat slightly, simmer 15 minutes or until all liquid is absorbed and peaches are soft. Add the butter and marshmallows, stir until melted and mixture is smooth. Remove from heat; cool slightly.
3 Spread coconut and oatmeal on an oven tray. Toast under a hot grill for 5 minutes (be careful not to allow coconut to burn). Transfer peach mixture to food processor bowl; add milk powders, coconut and oatmeal. Using the pulse action, press the button for 15 seconds or until the mixture is smooth.
4 Spoon the mixture into the prepared tin; smooth surface with a wet hand. Refrigerate for 2 hours or until set.
5 When set, remove from tin and peel off foil. Using a sharp knife cut into bars. Roll the bars in the extra coconut. Store Coconut Peach Bars in an airtight container between layers of greaseproof paper for up to 2 weeks.

Coconut Peach Bars (top),
Apricot and Gingernut Logs (bottom).

Chocolate-Coated Nougat

Preparation time:
  1 hour
Cooking time:
  30 minutes +
  overnight refrigeration
Makes 80

1½ cups sugar
⅓ cup golden syrup
¾ cup liquid glucose
2 tablespoons malt
  extract
2 tablespoons water
2 eggs, separated
60 g butter
200 g dark compound
  chocolate

1 Line base and sides of a shallow 18 x 27 cm oblong cake tin with foil. Brush foil with melted butter or oil.
2 Combine the sugar, syrup, glucose, malt and water in a large heavy-based pan. Stir over medium heat without boiling until sugar has completely dissolved. Brush crystals from the side of the pan with a wet pastry brush. Bring to the boil, reduce heat slightly and boil without stirring for 15-20 minutes; OR until a teaspoon of mixture dropped into cold water reaches hard-ball stage (see page 3); OR if using a sugar thermometer it must reach 122°C (see page 3). Remove from heat immediately.
3 Place egg whites in a large dry mixer bowl. Using electric beaters, beat whites until firm peaks form. Add one quarter of the hot syrup in a thin stream, beating constantly until mixture is thick and glossy; about 5 minutes.
4 Return the remaining syrup to heat. Bring to boil, reduce heat slightly and boil syrup without stirring for 5-10 minutes; OR until a teaspoon of mixture dropped into cold water reaches hard-crack stage (see page 3); OR if using a sugar thermometer it must reach 154°C (see page 3). Remove from heat immediately. Add remaining syrup to egg mixture in a thin stream, beating constantly until mixture is thick. Add egg yolks and butter, beat until well combined.
5 Pour mixture into the prepared tin; smooth surface. Freeze until set, preferably overnight. When set, remove from tin and cut into even pieces with a sharp knife dipped in hot water.
6 Line a biscuit tray with greaseproof paper. Place the chocolate in a medium heatproof bowl. Stand over a pan of simmering water, stir until the chocolate has melted and is smooth. Cool slightly (see Note). Using two forks and working quickly, dip the nougat pieces one at a time into chocolate to coat. Lift out, drain off excess chocolate and place on prepared tray. Refrigerate 30 minutes or until set. Store in an airtight container in a cool, dry place for up to 7 days.

Note: Ensure chocolate is not so hot that it will melt the nougat.

Nutty Clusters

Preparation time:
  20 minutes + 30
  minutes refrigeration
Cooking time:
  10 minutes
Makes 20

125 g dark cooking
  chocolate, chopped
½ cup chopped mixed
  unsalted nuts

1 Line a baking tray with aluminium foil.
2 Place chocolate in a medium heatproof bowl. Stand over a pan of simmering water, stir until the chocolate has melted and is smooth. Add chopped nuts to the chocolate, stir until nuts are well coated. Remove from heat.
3 Drop heaped teaspoons of the mixture

Chocolate-Coated Nougat (top), Nutty Clusters (bottom).

onto the prepared tray.
Refrigerate 30 minutes
or until set. Store Nutty
Clusters in an airtight
container in a cool dark
place, or the refrigerator
in hot weather, for up
to 7 days.

Note: For more crunch,
toast the nuts before
adding to the melted
chocolate mixture.
Make Almond Clusters
by substituting slivered
almonds for mixed nuts
in this recipe.

HINT
To toast nuts, scatter
on a lightly greased
oven tray. Bake in
moderate 180°C oven
10 minutes or until
golden. Cool on tray.

Easy Chocolates

The chocolates in this chapter are as delicious to eat as they are simple to prepare. Yet the elegance of Chocolate Meringue Kisses or Chocolate Almond and Pistachio Cups will belie their easy preparation as they impress guests at your next dinner party.

Marbled Jaffa Thins

Preparation time:
15 minutes
Cooking time:
5 minutes
Makes 48

300 g *white chocolate*
melts
300 g *dark compound*
chocolate, chopped
4 *drops orange*
flavouring oil

1 Brush a 30 x 25 x 2 cm Swiss roll tin with melted butter or oil. Cover base with baking paper, extend paper out over two sides.
2 Place white chocolate melts in a medium heatproof bowl. Stand over pan of simmering water, stir until the chocolate has melted and is smooth. Cool slightly. Repeat this procedure with the dark chocolate. Add two drops of the orange oil to each bowl of chocolate; stir well.
3 Drop tablespoonfuls of melted chocolate into the prepared tin, alternating white and dark chocolates. Tip tin gently to spread the chocolate evenly to all sides. Using the blunt end of a wooden skewer, swirl chocolate to create a marbled effect. Leave to set.
4 Using sides of paper, carefully lift chocolate from tin. Gently peel off the paper. Using a sharp knife, cut into squares. Store the Marbled Jaffa Thins in an airtight container in a cool, dark place, or in the refrigerator in hot weather, up to 4 weeks.

Marbled Jaffa Thins (top), Dried Fruit Clusters (p. 36) (bottom).

Dried Fruit Clusters

Preparation time:
  10 minutes
Cooking time:
  5 minutes
Makes about 30

250 g dark cooking
  chocolate, chopped
300 g mixed dried fruit

1 Line a 32 x 28 cm
oven tray with foil.
2 Place chocolate in a
medium heatproof
bowl. Stand over pan of
simmering water, stir
until the chocolate has
melted and is smooth.
Cool slightly.
3 Add the dried fruit to
the melted chocolate
and stir well. Place level
tablespoons of mixture
onto the prepared tray.
Leave to set at room
temperature. Store in an
airtight container in a
cool, dark place, or the
refrigerator in hot
weather, up to 4 weeks.

HINT
Try this easy and
very grown-up hot
chocolate drink.
Melt 200 g good
quality dark or milk
chocolate. Stir into it
1 L hot milk laced
with ½ cup of rum,
brandy, or your
favourite liqueur.

Choc-dipped Marzipan Dates

Preparation time:
  20 minutes
Cooking time:
  5 minutes
Makes 20

2 tablespoons icing
  sugar
50 g marzipan
20 g slivered almonds
20 dates, pitted
200 g dark compound
  chocolate, chopped

1 Line a 32 x 28 cm
oven tray with foil.
2 Dust work surface
with icing sugar, and
knead marzipan and
almonds together. Roll
into a log shape 20 cm
long. Cut into 20 pieces.
3 Cut the dates in half
lengthways and
sandwich together with
a piece of marzipan.
Smooth with fingers to
re-form shape.
4 Place chocolate in a
small heatproof bowl.
Stand over pan of
simmering water, stir
until chocolate has
melted and is smooth.
Cool slightly. Using two
forks, carefully dip the
dates one at a time into
the chocolate to coat.
Lift out, drain excess
chocolate, then place on

prepared tray. Leave to
set. Store in an airtight
container in a cool, dark
place, or the refrigerator
in hot weather, for up to
4 weeks.

Ginger Bites

Preparation time:
  10 minutes
Cooking time:
  5 minutes
Makes about 18

200 g dark cooking
  chocolate, chopped
250 g glacé ginger
  cubes

1 Line a 32 x 28 cm
oven tray with foil.
2 Place chocolate in a
medium heatproof
bowl. Stand over a pan
of simmering water, stir
until chocolate has
melted and is smooth.
Cool slightly.
3 Add glacé ginger to
chocolate; stir well to
combine. Place heaped
tablespoons of mixture
onto the prepared tray.
Leave to set at room
temperature. Store in an
airtight container in a
cool, dark place, or the
refrigerator in hot
weather, up to 4 weeks.

Note: Crystallised
ginger is too sugary to
use in this recipe.

---

*Ginger Bites (top), Choc-dipped
Marzipan Dates (bottom).*

Liquorice Logs
Preparation time:
  20 minutes
Cooking time:
  10 minutes
Makes about 44

2 x 90 cm liquorice
  straps or pieces
150 g dark compound
  chocolate, chopped
60 g white chocolate
  melts

1 Line a 32 x 28 cm
oven tray with foil.
Cut the liquorice straps
into 4 cm pieces.
2 Place dark chocolate
in a medium heatproof
bowl. Stand over pan of
simmering water, stir
until the chocolate has
melted and is smooth.
Let cool slightly. Using
two forks, dip liquorice
pieces one at a time in
chocolate to coat.
Lift out, drain excess
chocolate, then place
onto the prepared tray.
Leave to set at room
temperature.
3 Place white chocolate
melts in a medium
heatproof bowl. Stand
over pan of simmering
water, stir until the
chocolate has melted
and is smooth. Cool
slightly. Drizzle or pipe
across logs to decorate.
Leave to set at room

temperature. Store
Liquorice Logs in an
airtight container in a
cool dark place, or the
refrigerator in hot
weather, up to 4 weeks.

Hedgehogs
Preparation time:
  20 minutes + 1 hour
  refrigeration
Cooking time:
  10 minutes
Makes 56

125 g unsalted butter
1/2 cup sugar
125 g plain biscuits,
  crushed
1 cup walnuts, chopped
1/2 cup cocoa
1 egg, beaten
125 g dark cooking
  chocolate, chopped

1 Line base and sides of
a shallow 27 x 18 cm
cake tin with foil,
extending foil over two
sides. Brush foil with
melted butter or oil.

2 Combine butter and
sugar in a large heavy-
based pan. Stir over
medium heat until the
butter has melted and
the sugar has dissolved.
3 Reduce heat; add the
crushed biscuits,
chopped walnuts and
cocoa; stir until well
combined. Remove
from heat and leave to
cool slightly. Pour in the
beaten egg (see Note),
and beat well with a
wooden spoon. Pour
the mixture into the
prepared tin and press
in firmly, using the back
of a metal spoon to
smooth the surface.
4 Place chocolate in a
small heatproof bowl.
Stand over a pan of
simmering water, stir
until the chocolate has
melted and is smooth.
Let cool slightly. Pour
over the biscuit base.
(Decorate with walnut
pieces if desired).
Refrigerate for 1 hour.
5 Using the foil,
carefully lift the slice
out of the tin. Using a
sharp knife, cut into
56 small squares. Store
Hedgehogs in an airtight
container in a cool,
dark place, or the
refrigerator in hot
weather, up to 2 weeks.

Note: Make sure the
biscuit and nut mixture
is not too hot when
adding the egg or it will
"cook" and form lumps.

Liquorice Logs (top), Hedgehogs (bottom).

1. For Chocolate Meringue Kisses: Add sugar gradually, beating constantly.

2. Pipe meringue in small stars onto the prepared trays.

Chocolate Meringue Kisses

Preparation Time:
 30 minutes
Cooking Time:
 1 hour + 10 minutes
Makes 36

3 egg whites
3/4 cup caster sugar
1/2 teaspoon white
 vinegar
1/4 teaspoon cream of
 tartar
60 g dark chocolate,
 chopped
20 g white vegetable
 shortening

1 Preheat oven to slow 120°C. Brush two 32 x 28 cm oven trays with melted butter or oil, line base with paper; grease paper.
2 Place egg whites in a small, dry mixing bowl (see Note). Using electric beaters, beat whites until soft peaks form.
3 Add sugar gradually, beating constantly until the mixture is thick and glossy and all the sugar is dissolved. Add the vinegar and cream of tartar; beat until well combined.
4 Spoon the mixture into a piping bag fitted with a fluted piping nozzle; pipe meringue in small stars onto the prepared trays. Bake for 1 hour or until the meringue is pale and crisp. Turn off oven; leave meringues inside to cool completely. Remove from oven.
5 Place the chocolate and shortening in a medium heatproof bowl. Stand over a pan of simmering water, stir until the chocolate has melted and the mixture is smooth. Leave the mixture to cool slightly.

6 Dip the meringue stars upside down into the chocolate mixture. Turn right side up and stand on a wire rack until chocolate has set. Store in an airtight container in a cool, dry place for up to 3 weeks.

Note: Make sure that the bowl you use for beating the meringue is absolutely clean. Even a tiny trace of grease will stop egg whites whipping.

HINT
Meringue should be white or just slightly coloured when cooked, with a crisp shell and soft centre. Serve promptly when combined with other ingredients, such as pastry cream or ice-cream, as it will begin to soften within an hour or two. Cooked meringues freeze well for up to 6 months.

Chocolate Meringue Kisses.

3. Melt chocolate and shortening in a medium heatproof bowl.

4. Dip meringue stars upside down into the chocolate mixture.

41

Choc-Honeycomb Pecan Bars

Preparation Time:
 25 minutes
Cooking Time:
 5 minutes
Makes 50

*200 g dark cooking
 chocolate, chopped
40 g honeycomb,
 roughly chopped
1/3 cup pecans, roughly
 chopped*

1 Line base and sides of a 26 x 8 x 4.5 cm bar tin with aluminium foil, extending the foil over two sides.
2 Place the chocolate in a medium heatproof bowl. Stand over a pan of simmering water, stir until the chocolate has melted and is smooth. Remove from heat. Add chopped honeycomb and pecans, stir gently until well coated with the chocolate.
3 Pour mixture into the prepared tin; smooth the surface. Refrigerate until set. When firm, lift out of tin using foil. Peel off foil and cut bar into very thin slices. Store in an airtight container in a cool, dry place, or in the refrigerator in hot weather, up to 2 weeks.

Chocolate Almond and Pistachio Cups

Preparation Time:
 50 minutes
Cooking Time:
 5 minutes
Makes 28

*150 g white chocolate
 melts
28 foil confectionery
 cases
100 g cream cheese,
 softened
2 tablespoons icing
 sugar, sifted
40 g butter, softened
2 tablespoons ground
 almonds
2 tablespoons ground
 pistachios
50 g dark chocolate,
 grated
extra grated dark
 chocolate, to decorate*

1 Place white chocolate melts in small heatproof bowl. Stand over pan of simmering water, stir until the chocolate has melted and is smooth.

Working one at a time, pour a teaspoon of melted chocolate into each confectionery case. Use a small brush to coat the inside with chocolate, making sure chocolate is thick and there are no gaps or holes. Turn upside down on a wire rack to set.
2 Beat cream cheese in small mixing bowl until smooth and creamy. Add sugar and butter, beating 2 minutes or until the mixture is smooth and fluffy. Using a metal spoon, fold in the nuts and the grated chocolate. Stir until well combined.
3 Carefully peel off foil from chocolate cases. Spoon the cream cheese mixture into a small piping bag fitted with a narrow, round nozzle. Pipe mixture in a swirl into cases. Sprinkle with extra grated chocolate. Store in an airtight container in the refrigerator up to 7 days.

> ### HINT
> Give a sophisticated finish to truffles, chocolate cakes or slices by sifting good quality cocoa powder over. For a sweeter taste mix the cocoa with an equal quantity of icing sugar or use drinking chocolate powder.

*Choc-Honeycomb Pecan Bars (top),
Chocolate Almond and Pistachio Cups (bottom).*

43

Macadamia Slice

Preparation time:
  20 minutes + 1 hour
  refrigeration
Cooking time:
  5 minutes
Makes 60

250 g packet plain
  biscuits, crushed
1 cup desiccated coconut
1/2 cup cocoa
1 1/4 cups (150 g) crushed
  macadamia nuts
400 g can condensed
  milk
60 g unsalted butter,
  melted
80 g white chocolate
  melts

1 Line base and sides
of a shallow 30 x 20 cm
oblong cake tin with
foil, extending over two
sides. Brush foil with
melted butter or oil.
2 Place the crushed
biscuits, coconut, cocoa
and macadamia nuts
into a large mixing
bowl. Make a well in
the centre and add the
condensed milk and
melted butter. Stir until
well combined.
3 Pour the mixture into
prepared tin and press
in firmly. Use the back
of a metal spoon to
smooth the surface.
Refrigerate the mixture
for 1 hour.

4 Place chocolate melts
in a small heatproof
bowl. Stand over pan of
simmering water, stir
until chocolate has
melted and mixture is
smooth. Cool slightly.
Drizzle or pipe the
chocolate in a lattice
pattern over the slice.
Leave to set at room
temperature. Using foil,
lift the base from the tin
and gently peel off foil.
Using a sharp knife, cut
into 60 small squares.
Store Macadamia Slices
in an airtight container
in a cool, dark place,
or the refrigerator in
hot weather, for up to
2 weeks.

Note: This recipe can
be made with pecans or
walnuts instead of
macadamias if liked.

Glacé Fruit Chocolates

Preparation Time:
  45 minutes
Cooking time:
  5 minutes
Makes 15

130 g glacé pears
130 g glacé peaches
100 g dark chocolate
  melts
50 g white chocolate
  melts

1 Line an oven tray
with greaseproof paper.
Cut each glacé fruit into
two or three pieces,
depending on size.
2 Place dark chocolate
melts in a small
heatproof bowl. Stand
over pan of simmering
water, stir until chocolate
has melted and is
smooth. Let cool slightly.
3 Half-dip fruits one at
a time into chocolate.
Drain off any excess
chocolate. Place onto
prepared tray. Leave to
set at room temperature.
4 Place white chocolate
melts in a small
heatproof bowl. Stand
over pan of simmering
water, stir until the
chocolate has melted
and is smooth. Cool
slightly. Spoon into a
small paper icing bag,
seal open end. Snip tip
off bag, pipe white
chocolate in squiggles
over the dark chocolate.
Allow to set. Store in an
airtight container in a
cool, dry place for up to
3 weeks.

HINT
Presentation makes
all the difference.
Use small baskets or
boxes, lined with
scraps of satin or
lace, or even paper
doilies, to give a
special 'treasure
chest' touch to your
chocolates or sweets.

*Macadamia Slice (top), Glacé Fruit
Chocolates (bottom).*

Chocolate Pretzels (left), Chocolate Hazelnut Wafers (right).

Chocolate Pretzels

Preparation Time:
  25 minutes
Cooking Time:
  5 minutes
Makes about 20

*100 g dark chocolate
  melts*
*2 tablespoons demerara
  sugar*

1 Place dark chocolate melts in a medium heatproof bowl. Stand over pan of simmering water, stir until the chocolate has melted and is smooth. Leave to cool slightly.
2 Spoon chocolate into a small paper piping bag, seal open end. Snip tip off piping bag; pipe chocolate into curved and straight pretzel shapes onto a sheet of greaseproof paper.
3 Before chocolate sets, sprinkle with the sugar. Allow to set completely. Store in an airtight container in a cool, dry place for up to 4 weeks.

Note. Add a few drops of confectionery oil to flavour the chocolate if desired.

> **HINT**
> Make a sweetie salad for a child's party by mixing a variety of coloured sweets in a large bowl lined with lettuce-green tissue.

Chocolate Hazelnut Wafers

Preparation Time:
  45 minutes
Cooking Time:
  15 minutes
Makes 32

*200 g dark cooking
  chocolate, chopped*
*16 (4 x 6 cm) ice-cream
  wafers*
*1/4 cup chocolate
  hazelnut spread*
60 g butter
*1/4 cup ground
  hazelnuts or walnuts*

1 Line a baking tray with aluminium foil. Mark an 18 cm square onto the foil.

Coconut Roughs.

2 Place the chocolate in a medium heatproof bowl. Stand over a pan of simmering water, stir until the chocolate has melted and is smooth. Spread half the chocolate evenly over the marked square. Place 8 wafers over the chocolate to cover and press gently. Refrigerate until set.
3 Combine chocolate hazelnut spread, butter and ground nuts in a small pan. Stir over low heat until the butter has melted and mixture is smooth. Remove from heat; leave to cool slightly. Spread mixture evenly over wafer base. Cover with remaining wafers; gently press down. Spread the

remaining chocolate over the top of wafers. Refrigerate until set.
4 Using a sharp knife, cut into squares. Store Chocolate Hazelnut Wafers in an airtight container in a cool, dry place for up to 4 weeks.

Coconut Roughs

Preparation Time:
  25 minutes
Cooking Time:
  5 minutes
Makes 20

200 g milk chocolate melts
¾ cup desiccated coconut
¼ cup shredded coconut

1 Line a baking tray with aluminium foil.
2 Place chocolate melts in a medium heatproof bowl. Stand over pan of simmering water, stir until the chocolate has melted and is smooth. Add the desiccated coconut, stir until the mixture is well combined.
3 Place the shredded coconut on an oven tray under a hot grill for 5 minutes or until lightly golden.
4 Drop heaped teaspoons of chocolate mixture onto the prepared tray. Sprinkle with toasted coconut. Allow to set completely. Store in an airtight container in a cool, dry place for up to 4 weeks.

Special Occasion Chocolates

S ometimes you really want to knock their socks off. These chocolates will cost you a little time and concentration to prepare, but the results are worth the effort. For a spectacular finale to a dinner party, serve a platter of three or four types of chocolates matched with fine coffee and the best liqueur.

Chocolate Truffles

Preparation time:
  15 minutes + 1 hour
  refrigeration
Cooking time:
  5 minutes
Makes about 40

300 g dark cooking
  chocolate, chopped
90 g unsalted butter
1/2 cup cream
2 tablespoons brandy
cocoa, to coat

1 Place chocolate in a medium mixing bowl. Combine butter and cream in a small heavy-based pan; stir over low heat until the butter has melted. Bring to boil; remove from heat. Pour the hot cream mixture over chocolate. Using a wooden spoon, stir until chocolate has melted and mixture is smooth. Stir in the brandy.
2 Cool mixture in the refrigerator, stirring occasionally. When firm enough to handle, roll heaped teaspoons of the mixture into balls.
3 Sift cocoa onto greaseproof paper. Roll each truffle in cocoa until generously coated. Refrigerate until firm. Store Truffles in an airtight container in the refrigerator for up to 2 weeks.

Note: You may have finger marks on truffles after rolling in cocoa. To remove marks, re-roll close to serving time.

Clockwise from left: Chocolate Orange Swirls, Chocolate Truffles and Strawberry Hearts (p. 50).

1. For Strawberry Hearts: Combine sugar, cream, glucose and glycerine in pan.

2. Beat mixture for 8 minutes until thick and opaque.

Strawberry Hearts

Preparation time:
  15 minutes
Cooking time:
  30 minutes
Makes about 35

1 1/2 cups sugar
2/3 cup cream
1/4 cup glucose syrup
1 tablespoon glycerine
2 teaspoons strawberry
  flavouring
4 drops red food
  colouring
300 g dark compound
  chocolate, chopped

1 Combine the sugar, cream, glucose and glycerine in a medium, heavy-based pan. Stir over medium heat without boiling until sugar has completely dissolved. Brush sugar crystals from sides of pan with a wet pastry brush. Bring to the boil, reduce heat slightly, boil without stirring for 15 minutes; OR boil until a teaspoon of mixture dropped into cold water reaches soft-ball stage (see page 3); OR if using a sugar thermometer it must reach 115°C (see page 3). Remove from heat immediately and place pan on a wooden board.
2 Add flavouring and colouring. Using electric beaters, beat mixture for 8 minutes, until thick and opaque. Turn onto work surface lightly dusted with cornflour; knead until smooth. Leave to cool completely.
3 Roll the fondant out to 1 cm thickness. Cut into shapes using a small heart-shaped biscuit cutter (about 4 cm across).
4 Line a tray with foil. Place the chocolate in a medium heatproof bowl. Stand over pan of simmering water, stir until chocolate has melted and is smooth.

Cool slightly. Using two forks, carefully dip hearts one at a time in chocolate to coat. Lift out, drain off excess chocolate and place onto prepared tray. Leave to set. Store Strawberry Hearts in an airtight container in a cool, dark place for up to 2 weeks.

Chocolate Orange Swirls

Preparation time:
  20 minutes + 2 hours refrigeration
Cooking time:
  5 minutes
Makes 48

125 g dark cooking
  chocolate, chopped
90 g unsalted butter
2 cups sifted icing sugar
4 egg yolks
1 teaspoon finely grated
  orange rind
48 paper or foil
  confectionery cases

3. Using a rolling pin, roll fondant out to 1 cm thickness.

4. Using two forks, dip hearts one at a time in melted chocolate.

1 Combine chocolate and butter in a small, heavy-based pan. Stir over very low heat until melted and mixture is combined. Remove from heat. Transfer to a medium mixing bowl.

2 Using a wooden spoon, gradually stir in icing sugar. Add the egg yolks, one at a time, beating thoroughly after each addition. Beat in the orange rind. Refrigerate mixture until firm enough to shape, about 2 hours.

3 Spoon the mixture into a piping bag fitted with a star tube. Pipe into small paper or foil confectionery cases. Refrigerate until firm. Store Chocolate Orange Swirls in an airtight container in refrigerator for up to 3 days.

Note: Confectionery cases are available from specialty kitchenware or cake-decorating stores.

Vienna Cups

Preparation time:
  25 minutes + 30 minutes setting
Cooking time:
  15 minutes
Makes 16

80 g dark compound chocolate, chopped
16 foil confectionery cases
80 g milk chocolate melts
2 tablespoons cream
1 teaspoon instant coffee powder
60 g white chocolate, chopped
drinking chocolate, for dusting

1 Place dark chocolate in a small heatproof bowl. Stand over pan of simmering water, stir until the chocolate has melted and mixture is smooth. Cool slightly. Working one at a time, pour a teaspoon of melted chocolate into each confectionery case. Use a small brush to coat the inside with chocolate, making sure the chocolate is thick and there are no gaps. Turn cases upside down on a wire rack to set.

2 Place milk chocolate melts in a small mixing bowl. Combine cream and coffee powder in a small heavy-based pan; stir over low heat until combined. Bring to the boil; remove from heat. Pour hot cream mixture over chocolate. Using a wooden spoon, stir until the chocolate has melted and mixture is smooth. Set aside to cool.

3 Place a teaspoon of the cooled coffee mixture into each chocolate case.

4 Place white chocolate in a small heatproof bowl. Stand over a pan of simmering water, stir until chocolate has melted. Leave to cool until it is almost re-set, stirring occasionally. Spoon ½ teaspoons of white chocolate onto the coffee mixture, leaving surface rough. Leave to set. Peel off foil, sprinkle drinking chocolate powder lightly over each case. Store Vienna Cups in an airtight container in the refrigerator for up to 2 weeks.

Brandy Twigs
Preparation time:
  20 minutes
Cooking time:
  5 minutes
Makes 25

100 g marzipan
1 tablespoon brandy
125 g dark compound
  chocolate, chopped

1 Line a 32 x 28 cm oven tray with foil.
2 Press the marzipan out to a flat disc shape. Place into a medium mixing bowl and add the brandy. Work the marzipan with your hands to incorporate brandy into it.
3 On a wooden board, roll out the marzipan into a log-shape 25 cm long. Cut into 25 equal pieces. Using the flat of your hand, roll each piece into a twig shape, about 6 cm long.
4 Place chocolate in a medium heatproof bowl.

Stand over a pan of simmering water, stir until the chocolate has melted and is smooth. Cool slightly. Using fingers, dip twigs one at a time into the melted chocolate. Lift out and drain excess chocolate. Place on prepared tray to set, making sure the twigs are not touching. Store Brandy Twigs in an airtight container in a cool dark place, or in the refrigerator in hot weather, up to 4 weeks.

Note: In this recipe, brandy can be replaced with your favourite spirit.

Hazelnut Truffles
Preparation time:
  25 minutes + 1 hour
  refrigeration
Cooking time:
  10 minutes
Makes 30

125 g milk chocolate
  melts
50 g unsalted butter
2 tablespoons cream
50 g ground hazelnuts
250 g dark compound
  chocolate, chopped
30 hazelnut halves

1 Place milk chocolate melts in a small mixing bowl. Combine the cream and butter in a

small heavy-based pan; stir over low heat until butter has melted. Bring to the boil. Remove from heat and pour hot cream mixture over the chocolate melts. Using a wooden spoon, stir until chocolate has melted and mixture is smooth. Add ground hazelnuts; mix well.
3 Cool in refrigerator for 15 minutes or until firm enough to handle, stirring occasionally. Roll level tablespoons of mixture into balls. Return to refrigerator for a further 15 minutes or until firm.
4 Line a 32 x 28 cm oven tray with foil. Place dark chocolate in a medium heatproof bowl. Stand over a pan of simmering water, stir until the chocolate has melted and is smooth. Let cool slightly. Using two forks, dip the truffles one at a time into the chocolate to coat. Lift out, drain excess chocolate, then place onto the prepared tray. Working quickly, press a hazelnut half onto each truffle before chocolate hardens. Refrigerate for 30 minutes to set. Store Hazelnut Truffles in an airtight container in the refrigerator for up to 2 weeks.

Clockwise from left: Brandy Twigs, Hazelnut Truffles and Vienna Cups (p. 51).

Tiramisu Bites.

Tiramisu Bites

Preparation time:
 15 minutes + 20
 minutes refrigeration
Cooking time:
 10 minutes
Makes 24

6 large Italian-style
 sponge fingers
50 g milk chocolate
 melts
2 tablespoons cream
1/2 teaspoon instant
 coffee powder
1 1/2 teaspoons rum
200 g dark compound
 chocolate, chopped

1 Line a 32 x 28 cm
oven tray with foil.

2 Trim rounded ends
from sponge fingers.
Cut each finger into
4 even pieces. Place
milk chocolate melts
into a small mixing
bowl. Combine cream
and coffee powder in a
small heavy-based pan;
stir over low heat until
the coffee powder has
dissolved. Bring to the
boil, remove from heat.
Pour hot cream mixture
over chocolate. Using a
wooden spoon stir until
chocolate has melted
and the mixture is
smooth. Stir in rum.
3 Cool in refrigerator,
stirring occasionally, for
about 20 minutes. Cut
each sponge finger piece

in half horizontally,
spread generously with
cooled chocolate
mixture and sandwich
back together. Smooth
filling around edges.
4 Place dark chocolate
in a medium heatproof
bowl. Stand over a pan
of simmering water, stir
until the chocolate has
melted and is smooth.
Cool slightly. Using two
forks, dip the sponge
finger pieces one at a
time in chocolate to coat.
Lift out, drain excess
chocolate, then place
onto prepared tray to
set. Store Tiramisu Bites
in an airtight container
in a cool dark place for
up to 3 days.

Lemon Truffles.

Lemon Truffles

Preparation time:
20 minutes + 1 hour
refrigeration
Cooking time:
5 minutes
Makes about 15

200 g *white chocolate,*
chopped
1/4 cup *cream*
30 g *butter*
25 g *plain sponge cake*
crumbs
1 teaspoon *finely grated*
lemon rind
50 g *white chocolate,*
extra, grated

1 Line a 32 x 28 cm
oven tray with foil.

2 Place chocolate in a
small mixing bowl.
Combine the cream and
butter in a small heavy-
based pan; stir over low
heat until butter has
melted. Bring to the
boil; remove from heat.
Pour hot cream mixture
over chocolate. Using a
wooden spoon, stir
until the chocolate has
melted and mixture is
smooth. Stir in the cake
crumbs and lemon rind.
3 Cool in refrigerator
for 30 minutes, stirring
occasionally, until firm
enough to handle. Roll
heaped teaspoons of the
mixture into balls.
4 Spread the grated
chocolate onto a sheet

of greaseproof paper.
Roll each truffle in the
grated chocolate until
generously coated, then
place onto prepared
tray. Refrigerate for
30 minutes or until firm.
Store Lemon Truffles in
an airtight container in
the refrigerator for up
to 2 weeks.

> **HINT**
> Decorate home-made
> chocolates with
> sugared violets for an
> old-fashioned look.
> When dipping your
> chocolates, leave a
> swirl of extra
> chocolate across the
> top for a rich finish.

Chocolate Orange Peel Candies

Preparation time:
  40 minutes +
  overnight standing
Cooking time:
  30 minutes
Makes about 48

3 *medium oranges*
1 *cup sugar*
1 *cup water*
1 *teaspoon lemon juice*
200 g *dark compound chocolate, chopped*

1 Cut the oranges into quarters and remove peel. Discard the flesh. Scrape all the white pith from peel; cut each quarter lengthways into 1 cm strips.
2 Place orange peel in a small heavy-based pan, cover with water. Bring to boil; remove from heat. Drain the peel thoroughly, then return to pan. Repeat this boiling process twice more. Pat peel dry with absorbent paper.
3 Combine the sugar, water and lemon juice in a medium heavy-based pan. Stir over medium heat without boiling until sugar has completely dissolved. Add peel. Bring to boil, reduce heat slightly, boil without stirring for 15 minutes or until the peel is translucent.

Remove pan from heat immediately.
4 Drain peel. Place on wire rack covered with a sheet of foil. Leave overnight to dry at room temperature.
5 Place the chocolate in a medium heatproof bowl. Stand over pan of simmering water, stir until the chocolate has melted and is smooth. Cool slightly. Using two forks, dip peel pieces one at a time into chocolate to coat. Lift out, drain excess chocolate, then place on a sheet of greaseproof paper to set. Store in an airtight container in a cool, dry place for up to 4 weeks.

Note: Try replacing the orange peel and dark chocolate with lemon peel and white chocolate in this recipe.

HINT
If you have any warm chocolate left over after dipping centres, stir in chopped nuts, raisins, muesli or whatever you have to hand. Drop spoonfuls of the mixture onto greaseproof paper or foil and leave to set. Or dip one half of shortbread or wholewheat biscuits into the chocolate and leave to set.

Hazelnut Crisp Truffles

Preparation time:
  30 minutes + 30
  minutes refrigeration
Cooking time:
  10 minutes
Makes 20

100 g *dark cooking chocolate, chopped*
1/4 *cup cream*
50 g *unsalted butter*
1/4 *cup chocolate hazelnut spread*
20 (50 g) *whole hazelnuts*
3/4 *cup Rice Bubbles, lightly crushed*
50 g *hazelnuts, extra, roughly chopped*
150 g *dark cooking chocolate, extra, chopped*
30 g *white vegetable shortening*

1 Place chocolate in a medium mixing bowl. Combine cream, butter and hazelnut spread in a small heavy-based pan; stir over low heat until butter has melted. Bring to boil; remove from heat immediately. Pour hot cream mixture over the chocolate. Using a wooden spoon, stir until chocolate has melted and the mixture is smooth.
2 Cool in refrigerator for 15 minutes or until mixture is firm. Roll out

Hazelnut Crisp Truffles (left), Chocolate Orange Peel Candies (right).

level tablespoons of mixture; place a whole hazelnut in the centre and roll into balls, making sure nut is completely covered. Roll the truffles in the combined Rice Bubbles and chopped hazelnuts. Refrigerate 15 minutes or until firm.

3 Line a 32 x 28 cm oven tray with foil. Place the extra chocolate and shortening in a small heatproof bowl. Stand over a pan of simmering water, stir until the chocolate has melted and mixture is smooth; remove from heat. Leave to cool slightly.

4 Using two forks, dip truffles one at a time into chocolate mixture to coat. Lift out, drain excess chocolate, then place onto prepared tray to set. Store the Hazelnut Crisp Truffles in an airtight container in the refrigerator for up to 2 weeks.

57

1. For Irish Cream Cups: Pipe 3 or 4 dots on the base of each foil case.

2. Use a small brush to coat the inside of cases with chocolate.

Irish Cream Cups

Preparation time:
  1 hour
Cooking time:
  10 minutes
Makes 28

40 g white chocolate,
  chopped
28 foil confectionery
  cases
50 g dark chocolate
  melts
1/4 cup sugar
2 tablespoons water
1/4 cup Irish cream
  liqueur

1 Place white chocolate in a small heatproof bowl. Stand over a pan of simmering water, stir until the chocolate has melted and is smooth. Spoon chocolate into a small paper icing bag, seal open end. Snip tip off bag; pipe 4 dots or a spiral onto the base of each foil case. Leave to set at room temperature.
2 Place chocolate melts in a small heatproof bowl. Stand over a pan of simmering water, stir until the chocolate has melted and is smooth. Working one at a time, pour a teaspoon of melted chocolate into each confectionery case. Use a small brush to coat the inside with chocolate, making sure the chocolate is thick and there are no gaps. Turn case upside down on a wire rack to set.
3 Spread the remaining chocolate over a piece of foil to about 2 mm thick. When chocolate has nearly set, cut out 28 discs, about 2 cm wide, to fit as bases for the chocolate cups.
4 Combine sugar and water in a small heavy-based pan. Stir over low heat without boiling until the sugar has completely dissolved. Brush any sugar crystals from the side of the pan with a wet pastry brush. Bring to the boil, reduce heat slightly, boil without stirring for 10 minutes. Remove pan from heat. Leave to cool. Brush inside each of the chocolate cups with the cooled syrup.
5 Fill each cup 3/4 full with the Irish cream liqueur. Re-melt any chocolate remaining from discs. Spoon into a small paper icing bag, seal open end. Snip tip off bag. Carefully pipe around the edge of a cup. Place a disc on top and press gently to seal completely and prevent any liqueur leaking out. Repeat process until all cups are sealed. When set, peel off the foil. Store Irish Cream Cups in an airtight container in a cool, dry place for up to 2 weeks.

Irish Cream Cups.

3. Cut out 28 discs about 2 cm wide, to fit as bases for the chocolate cups.

4. Carefully pipe around edge of cup with melted chocolate; place disc on top to seal.

Layered Truffles

Preparation time:
  1½ hours
Cooking time:
  15-20 minutes
Makes 72

Truffle Base & Top
*250 g dark coooking
  chocolate, chopped*

Dark Layer
*200 g dark cooking
  chocolate, chopped
¼ cup cream
80 g unsalted butter*

White Layer
*130 g white chocolate,
  chopped
2 tablespoons cream
40 g unsalted butter*

1 Turn a 30 x 20 cm oblong cake tin upside down. Cover base of tin with alumnium foil.
2 To make Truffle Base: Place chocolate in a medium heatproof bowl. Stand over pan of simmering water, stir until the chocolate has melted and is smooth. Cool slightly. Spread half the chocolate over the base of the tin. Refrigerate 10 minutes, or until set. Set aside remaining chocolate.
3 To make Dark Layer: Place the chocolate in a medium mixing bowl. Combine the cream and butter in a small heavy-based pan. Stir over low heat until butter has melted. Bring to boil; remove from heat. Pour the hot cream mixture over chocolate. Using a wooden spoon, stir until chocolate has melted and mixture is smooth. Spread half the mixture evenly over the set chocolate. Return to refrigerator to set. Place remaining mixture in refrigerator to semi-set.
4 To make White Layer: Place the white chocolate in a medium mixing bowl. Combine cream and butter in a small, heavy-based pan. Stir over low heat until butter has melted. Bring to boil; remove from heat. Pour the hot cream mixture over chocolate. Using a wooden spoon, stir until chocolate has melted and mixture is smooth. Spread the mixture evenly over the set layers. Return to refrigerator to set.
5 Using electric beaters, beat remaining Dark Layer mixture until thick and creamy. Spread mixture evenly over the white chocolate layer. Return to refrigerator until set. Spread the remaining melted chocolate over the top. Leave to set completely.
6 When firm, cut into small squares with a long sharp knife.
Store Layered Truffles between sheets of greaseproof paper, in an airtight container in a cool, dry place, or in the refrigerator in hot weather, up to 4 weeks.

Mint Patties

Preparation time:
  1 hour
Cooking time:
  15 minutes
Makes 36

*1½ cups sugar
⅔ cup milk
¼ cup liquid glucose
1 tablespoon glycerine
2 teaspoons peppermint
  essence
green food colouring
250 g dark cooking
  chocolate, chopped
20 g white vegetable
  shortening*

1 Combine sugar, milk, glucose and glycerine in a medium heavy-based pan. Stir over medium heat without boiling until the sugar has completely dissolved. Bring to the boil and reduce heat slightly Boil without stirring for 15 minutes; OR boil until a teaspoon of mixture dropped into cold water reaches soft-ball stage (see page 3); OR if using a sugar thermometer it must reach 115°C (see page 3). Remove from heat immediately. Stir in the essence and colouring.

Mint Patties (top), Layered Truffles (bottom).

2 Transfer the mixture to a medium heatproof mixing bowl. Using electric beaters, beat until mixture thickens and turns opaque. Turn out onto work surface lightly dusted with icing sugar. Knead mixture for 2-3 minutes or until smooth. Roll out to about 1 cm thick. Cut into rounds using a 3 cm biscuit cutter. Dip the cutter in cornflour to prevent sticking.

3 Place chocolate and shortening in a medium heatproof bowl. Stand over pan of simmering water, stir until the chocolate has melted and mixture is smooth. Cool slightly. Using two forks, dip the mint patties one at a time into chocolate to coat. Lift out, drain excess chocolate, then place on a sheet of greaseproof paper to set at room temperature. Store Mint Patties in an airtight container in a cool, dry place for up to 3 weeks.

Note: The Mint Patty mixture can be made ahead. Store, covered in plastic wrap, up to 2 weeks in the refrigerator. When ready to serve, cut into rounds and follow Step 3 of recipe to coat with chocolate.

Choc-Dipped Brandy Snaps with Pecan Butter Cream

Preparation time:
  1 hour
Cooking time:
  40 minutes
Makes 32

Brandy Snaps
50 g butter
1/4 cup brown sugar
2 tablespoons golden syrup
1/4 cup plain flour, sifted
2 teaspoons ground ginger

Pecan Butter Cream
80 g unsalted butter
1/4 cup icing sugar, sifted
1 egg yolk
1 teaspoon vanilla essence
1/2 cup ground pecans

100 g dark cooking chocolate, for dipping

1 Preheat oven to moderate 180°C. Brush two 32 x 28 cm oven trays with melted butter or oil.
2 Combine the butter, sugar and syrup in a small heavy-based pan. Stir over low heat until the butter has melted and sugar completely dissolved. Remove from heat; add flour and ground ginger. Stir until well combined and mixture is smooth.

3 Drop teaspoons of the mixture onto prepared trays, two on each tray, to allow plenty of room for spreading. Bake for 5 minutes or until the mixture has spread and browned slightly. Leave for 30 seconds on tray. Using a metal spatula, carefully lift off brandy snaps. While still warm, roll around the handle of a wooden spoon into a cylinder shape. When cool and crisp, remove from handle and place on a wire rack to cool completely. Repeat with remaining mixture.
4 To make Pecan Butter Cream: Beat butter in small mixing bowl until light and creamy. Add sugar, beating 2 minutes or until the mixture is smooth and fluffy. Stir in vanilla essence and pecans. Mix until well combined. Spoon the mixture into a small piping bag fitted with a narrow round nozzle. Pipe mixture into the centre of Brandy Snaps.
5 Place the chocolate in small heatproof bowl. Stand over a pan of simmering water, stir until chocolate has melted and is smooth. Cool slightly. Dip each end of Brandy Snaps into chocolate, drain off excess chocolate, and place on a sheet of greaseproof paper to set. Store Brandy Snaps

in an airtight container in the freezer for up to 4 weeks. Serve directly from freezer; thawing is not necessary.

Note: Brandy Snaps can also be frozen unfilled and filled with Pecan Butter Cream or fresh whipped cream just before serving.

White Chocolate Apricot Balls

Preparation time:
  40 minutes + 15 minutes refrigeration
Cooking time:
  10 minutes
Makes 32

100 g dried apricots
1 tablespoon lemon juice
1 tablespoon brown sugar
1 teaspoon grated lemon rind
1/2 cup cream
125 g cream cheese, softened
100 g white chocolate, chopped
1/2 cup desiccated coconut, toasted
1/4 cup grated white chocolate

1 Combine the apricots, juice, sugar, lemon rind and cream in a medium heavy-based pan. Stir over low heat until the sugar has completely

Choc-Dipped Brandy Snaps with Pecan Butter Cream (top),
White Chocolate Apricot Balls (bottom).

dissolved. Bring to boil, reduce heat slightly, simmer 10-15 minutes or until all liquid is absorbed and apricots are soft. Remove from heat; cool slightly.

2 Using electric beaters, beat cream cheese in a medium bowl until light and creamy. Add apricot mixture, beating for 3 minutes or until the mixture is fairly smooth.

3 Place chocolate in a small heatproof bowl. Stand over a pan of simmering water, stir until the chocolate has melted and is smooth. Leave to cool slightly.

4 Add melted chocolate to the apricot mixture, beating for 1 minute or until mixture is smooth. Refrigerate 15 minutes or until mixture begins to firm.

5 In a medium mixing bowl combine the coconut and the grated chocolate. Roll heaped teaspoons of apricot mixture into balls. Roll balls in the coconut mixture, place on a tray and refrigerate until firm. Store White Chocolate Apricot Balls in an airtight container in a cool, dry place for up to 4 weeks.

Index